THE STONES OF EMPTINESS

ANTHONY THWAITE

The Stones of Emptiness

POEMS 1963-66

LONDON
OXFORD UNIVERSITY PRESS
NEW YORK   TORONTO
1967

*Oxford University Press, Ely House, London W.*1.

GLASGOW NEW YORK TORONTO MELBOURNE WELLINGTON
CAPE TOWN SALISBURY IBADAN NAIROBI LUSAKA ADDIS ABABA
BOMBAY CALCUTTA MADRAS KARACHI LAHORE DACCA
KUALA LUMPUR HONG KONG TOKYO

Printed in Great Britain by
The Bowering Press, Plymouth

For Ann again

CONTENTS

ACKNOWLEDGEMENTS

ACKNOWLEDGEMENTS are due to the following periodicals and anthologies in which some of these poems have previously appeared:

Best Poems of 1965, Critical Quarterly, The Listener, The London Magazine, New Statesman, New York Times, The New Yorker, New Poems 1965, The Observer, Rising Early, Spectator, Stand and *The Times Literary Supplement.*

'The Pond' (page 9) is © The New Yorker Magazine, Inc.

Acknowledgements are also due to the B.B.C. Third Programme for poems which have been broadcast in 'New Poetry', 'The Poet's Voice', and 'Poetry Now'.

LEAVINGS

I

EMPTYING the teapot out
Into the drain, I catch sight
Suddenly of flies at work
On some rubbish by the back
Of the shed, and standing there
Smell the small corruption where
A fishbone makes its measured path
Into the leaves, into the earth.

II

Under the raspberry canes I prod to light
Two Roman sherds, a glint of Roman glass,
A bit of bellarmine, some stoneware scraps,
And searching on might find the rougher wares,
Friable, gritty, Saxon: porous stuff
That lets the rain leak through, the dew absorb,
Frost craze and crack. *Frango*, I break, becomes
Fragment, the broken pieces to be joined
To give a date to everything we own.

III

The little duchess, aged four hundred, stirs
To feel the instruments break through the lead.
Troy stands on the nine layers of its filth
And I tread out another cigarette.

IV

Compost of feasts and leavings, thick
Layer after layer of scourings, peelings, rinds,
Bone pressed on potsherd, fish-head sieved to dust,

1

And in the spoil-heaps goes the fly, the quick
Mouse with her pink brood, and the maggot, slow
To render down the fat. Trash, husk, and rust,
Grass sickled, scythed, and mown, hedge-clippings, leaves,
Wet infiltrations, skins and rags of skins,
Humus of twigs and insects, skeletons
Of petals.
　　　　　Stale loaves and fishes so divided out
They feed five thousand trees, five million roots.

V

Pipes void it to the sea,
The Thames chokes on its way.
We live on what we spend,
Are spent, are lived upon.
Nothing has an end.
The compost is my son,
My daughter breeds the dust,
We become ash, air,
Water, earth, the past
Our daughters' sons share.

AT PAGHAM HARBOUR

THESE are salt acres, the sea's tithes
Drenched twice a day, worked by the crab and gull.
At low tide mud heaves and breathes
But only in waiting for the levelling pull
Each wave makes as it fills the harbour mouth.
Coarse grasses stand
Stiff before even the strongest wind.
No hedges here, or walls, or any path
Except the birds' frail tracks,
The scribbled spoors of crabs, and scattered rocks.

No one can tell the way the paths
Ran once, and who has walked them, over there
To Manhood, maybe, where the water bathes
Its buried church. The sea smothers the air
And we breathe salt and hear only the sea.
I think about
That nineteenth-century parson who looked out
And saw a wall of water half-fill his sky,
The sea marking its bounds,
Breaking its barriers, inheriting its lands.

AT DUNWICH

FIFTEEN churches lie here
Under the North Sea;
Forty-five years ago
The last went down the cliff.
You can see, at low tide,
A mound of masonry
Chewed like a damp bun.

In the village now (if you call
Dunwich a village now,
With a handful of houses, one street,
And a shack for Tizer and tea)
You can ask an old man
To show you the stuff they've found
On the beach when there's been a storm:

Knife-blades, buckles and rings,
Enough coins to fill an old sock,
Badges that men wore
When they'd been on pilgrimage,
Armfuls of broken pots.
People cut bread, paid cash,
Buttoned up against the cold.

Fifteen churches, and men
In thousands working at looms,
And wives brewing up stews
In great grey cooking pots.
I put out a hand and pull
A sherd from the cliff's jaws.
The sand trickles, then falls.

Nettles grow on the cliffs
In clumps as high as a house.
The houses have gone away.

Stand and look at the sea
Eating the land as it walks
Steadily treading the tops
Of fifteen churches' spires.

BLUE-DASH CHARGER

ADAM and Eve on a dish:
1680 or so: Bristol-made.
It hangs in the kitchen, a thing
We prize for its strangeness, age,
And maybe because it's rare.
It cost me a week's work.

With simple inherited skill,
No finesse but a crude delight,
Whoever painted its face
In green, yellow, blue, and brown
Knew what the job in hand was.
He had a surface to fill.

Adam, in curly brown wig,
Round-bellied, long-buttocked, holds out
One hand: the other is raised
Perhaps in doubt, or perhaps
Simply to balance the stance
Of the woman who shares the design—

Eve, breasts scooped by the brush,
Who stands with her long coarse hair
Swathed round such innocent parts
As the craftsman wished to suggest.
An apple in either hand,
Like a doll she waits with him there.

A leaf as big as his head
Is slapped across Adam's groin.
The snake, with a bull-calf's face,
Squints sideways down at the sight,
Nudging one apple Eve holds
With a blunt blue muzzle. The tree,

Where he grows as the only branch,
Is solid down to the earth
But the earth itself is one blur
Of blue, wiped, sponged, a mere trail
Dragged up to the blue-dashed rim.
The biggest fruit lie at the top.

Ungainly, this work, and not
Even with much new to say.
Such stories survive like this dish,
Childishly-done, with a chip
That might ruin the whole effect
But doesn't. A pure ornament,

An object for one who collects
Objects, it covers a span
More than its surface, a truth,
A myth, or a spoiled man's whim,
Anonymous innocence stuck
In an attitude, on a wall.

UNDERNEATH

From someone's transistor a quarter-mile away
The sound of someone's band lifts over gardens
And finds me here examining a weed
Trowelled up among hundreds in the patch of waste
At the end of this narrow bit of property
I own on the edge of London, where the clay
Starts one spade down, going as far below
As the roof of my house is high, and reaching water
Clear underneath, held in its caves and pockets,
Trapped, unevaporating, silent, cold,
But working back through roots and tall foundations
To mushroom up anywhere, now here
In the roots of the three-leafed weed I hold in my hand,
Disturbed for a moment by that distant band.

THE POND

WITH nets and kitchen sieves they raid the pond,
Chasing the minnows into bursts of mud,
Scooping and chopping, raking up frond after frond
Of swollen weed after a week of flood.

Thirty or forty minnows bob and flash
In every jam-jar hoarded on the edge,
While the shrill children with each ill-aimed splash
Haul out another dozen as they dredge.

Choked to its banks, the pond spills out its store
Of frantic life. Nothing can drain it dry
Of what it breeds: it breeds so effortlessly
Theft seems to leave it richer than before.

The nostrils snuff its rank bouquet—how warm,
How lavish, foul, and indiscriminate, fat
With insolent appetite and thirst, so that
The stomach almost heaves to see it swarm.

But trapped in glass the minnows flail and fall,
Sink, with upended bellies showing white.
After an hour I look and see that all
But four or five have died. The greenish light

Ripples to stillness, while the children bend
To spoon the corpses out, matter-of-fact,
Absorbed: as if creation's prodigal act
Shrank to this empty jam-jar in the end.

LESSON

In the big stockyards, where pigs, cows, and sheep
Stumble towards the steady punch that beats
All sense out of a body with one blow,
Certain old beasts are trained to lead the rest
And where they go the young ones meekly go.

Week after week these veterans show the way,
Then, turned back just in time, are led themselves
Back to the pens where their initiates wait.
The young must cram all knowledge in one day,
But the old who lead live on and educate.

HABIT

Solemn administrator, cowled creature
Ruling your lines in a book devised for
Recording our customs and our nature,

You impel such movements as keep us alive,
Eating, sleeping, always on the move
To the place where we must never arrive—

For that would be to break your rhythm,
Allowing us too easily to become
Mere animals of irregular stab and spasm.

Yet you are animal too: all of us know
That Pavlov's dog salivated for you,
That you tell the log-rolling elephant what he must do.

Patron of babies and the very old,
Adversary of clerks dreaming of Gauguin, shield
Of sergeant-majors doing what they are told:

Keep you as we may, singly or bunched together,
You grow into one hard carapace whatever
Soft twigs and shoots underneath wanly stir.

Put in compartments, like a honeycomb
You spill from cell to cell, leaving no room,
Stifling with sweet indulgence all who come

Prying or bustling, scouring with mop and rake.
On holiday, you are the last thing we take
But take you we do, and when it's over bring you back.

If we break you, we may get fat, grow young, go mad,
Wondering why we listened to what you said
Or wondering in the end whether you're all we've had.

Resented, you weigh us down like Atlas his world:
Cherished, you allow us without pain to grow old:
When we die, our children inherit you before we are cold.

THE RIGHT PLACE

Sardinia, 1964

In the distance a herd of goats
Jingles somewhere out of sight
In the clear September weather.
I lie on my back and make notes
About really nothing whatever,
Dazed with the heat and light.

How marvellous to make art
Out of stringing such things together!
Sea, ruins, limestone, bees,
Such emptiness, set apart
From the neat urbanities,
Under such a sky, in such weather.

A hare starts up from a bush,
Scattering berries about.
Eating figs warm from the tree,
Sensations jam in a rush.
Choked with ripe ecstasy
I stand on a mound and shout.

Already the mind's at work
Pretending to own this place,
Growing olives and grapes.
Think of the poems, the smoke
From my chimney drifting across
That valley of antique shapes!

The goat-bells come closer now,
And a man is rounding them up:
The only man here but me.
Well, anyway, that was how
It seemed for a moment. Now stop
Believing you're really free

Or would want to live here if you were.
The notes are just notes. The art
Is the art of what you can say.
The goatherd gives a long stare.
I say, '*Buon giorno*', and start
Back down the track, away.

TWO FACES

ONE gets inured to having the wrong face.
For years I thought it soft, too pink and young
To match that shrewd, mature, and self-possessed
Person behind it. In a forced grimace
I saw all that I *should* have been, the strong
Line linking nose to mouth, the net of care
Fixed by the concentration of the eyes.
Such marks upon the lineaments expressed
Things that I wanted most, but would not dare,
Prevented by the innocence I despised.

Yet now, this morning, as I change a blade,
Look up and clear the glass, I recognize
Some parody of that scored, experienced man.
But this one, as I take it, seems afraid
Of what he sees, is hesitant, with his eyes
Shifting away from something at my back.
No, this is not the one I recognized
Proleptically in mirrors; neither can
He any longer see what firm lines track
Back to that innocence he once despised.

PERSONAL EFFECTS

UNABLE to travel light, I carry
Unnecessary luggage here and there.
To live out of a suitcase, to be free
Of everything but a toothbrush and the fare—
Admirable, but I can't imagine how
Such people can ever have an anywhere
They call their own, and without that I know
Life would be a burden I couldn't bear.

So here, among the pyjamas and the socks,
I stow away a talisman or two,
And label that huge metal-lined travelling-box
Personal Effects, which may not seem true
Enough to convince the Customs, but is so.
An affluent magpie in a nest that creaks
With impedimenta, everywhere I go
I lug an accumulation of years or weeks.

Odd that a man with so much need of roots
Restlessly plucks them up, weighing a ton,
And finds that burdened travel somehow suits
His nature and his situation.
Naked we enter the world and naked we leave it,
So I have heard, and take it as true enough;
Yet no matter how reason and faith believe it,
Off I go, loaded with perishable stuff.

STREET SCENE: BENGHAZI

Two ram's horns married with a bit of gut
Wail on the pavement near the Sport Café
As Mustafa and I walk by the shut
Emporia this blue December Friday.

Mustafa wears a trim Italian suit,
Reads Sartre in the Faculty of Arts,
Writes poems behind dark glasses, is acute
About 'some' and 'any' and the various parts

Of speech. He will go far—maybe in Oil.
Whereas this flautist, swathed in motley shawls,
Unshaved, one-eyed, from whom the dogs recoil,
Seems at a dead end. Poverty appals

More when it sweetly insinuates and smiles.
Mustafa notices. 'A marabout', he says,
Explaining the presence: explanation reconciles.
I notice the moth-holes in the faded fez.

'That man is wise and holy', Mustafa says,
And puts a piastre in the wizened hand.
I avoid his glance. To Allah let there be praise.
Round Barclay's D.C.O. the armed guards stand.

THE WATCHERS

Out by Coefia
We walk across rock
And see the horizon
Twelve miles away,
Brown featureless hills
As the sun goes down
Casting in shadow
Only ourselves.

But we are noticed.
First two or three,
Then others, gather
On a slight mound
Where stones are heaped up
And white rags fly
Above a small boneyard.
They watch as we pass.

They call to each other
Like flurries of birds,
Laughing together
To see the pale strangers
So pointlessly walking
From nowhere to nowhere
Through rubble and thistles
With children and camera.

I raise my right hand
To greet them, but neither
We nor the watchers
Speak at that distance.
Neither guests nor trespassers
But simply strangers
Who have passed at a distance
This late afternoon.

Back in the car
I feel separateness dull me
And cannot connect
The road to the town,
Blinded in sunset,
With where the horizon
Is stained with the black
Power-station's smoke.

STILL LIFE

BREAD, olives, and dates. A bellied jug of water.
A red cloth spread out. A light in one corner.
So I compose the room, find it familiar.

The open window catches the evening breeze
Coming across the flecked ocean from Greece
Carrying the drift of eucalyptus trees.

These things to hand, the smell hanging like smoke,
I feel at home. The last stroke
Of the far cathedral's bell fell as you spoke

And with it caught the muezzin's braying call
In a strange discord, echoing in its fall
The Ramadan gun, the sound of festival.

But what is reconciled? The *tableau mort*
Is now no longer what my eyes once saw
Composed so firmly, shaped without a flaw.

Shape, colour, smell, familiar sounds and strange—
See how they meet and mingle, how they change,
And how they move away, quite out of range.

Always they elude me. Now my fingers stretch
Towards food, jug, cloth, light, objects within reach;
Static, composed; but foreign to my touch.

THE STONES OF EMPTINESS

Isaiah 34: 11

ERODED slabs, collapsed and weathered tables,
Porous and pocked limestone, rubble of schist:
They are the real blocks where the real foot stumbles,
Boulders where lizards move like Medusa's prey
Freed from their stone trance. Here the stone-eyed exist
Among pebbles, fossil-bearing images
Glaring their life-in-death in the blinding day.
At the dark cave's mouth they stand like effigies.

They define the void. They assert
How vast the distances are, featureless, bare.
Their absence creates the extremest kind of desert,
A sea of sand. They are to the desolate earth
What a single hawk is to the desolate air.
And suddenly here, grouped in a circle
In the middle of nowhere, they form a hearth
Round a fire long since dead, built by an unknown people.

The soil profitless under their strewn acres,
Even so they harbour in their ungenerous shade
Flowers as delicate as they themselves are fierce.
Scorpions entrench under them, flat as dry leaves.
In parched wadi beds, coagulate in a blockade
Against all but a man on foot, who, waterless
And far from home, stumbles as he perceives
Only that line of confusion, the stones of emptiness.

DUST

BEAUTIFUL only when the light catches it
Arrested yet volatile in a shaft of sun,
Or under the microscope, like an ancient detritus
Of snowflakes: otherwise valueless debris.
The ash from my cigarette, the air from my lungs,
The soles of my shoes, the palms of my hands, breed it,
Absorb it, carry it, disperse it. The liquids of bodies
Dry to it in the end, and the sea's salt.

Created from the beginning, it carries its beginnings
Even to the end. Metals and minerals
Are crushed to its substance: in the desert
It is beyond the harshness of sand. Soft,
Disposable, it collects in corners, to be moved
Only to another place: it cannot be moved
Finally. Indestructible, even in fire
It shapes its own phoenix, and rises with the wind.

Each second shifts it, animates its grey
Weight, bearing down on pliant surfaces.
Analyse its origins, and you find the full range
Of everything living and dead. It obeys water,
Lying down to a drenching, but as the sun
Parches that adversary it re-forms and spreads
Further and further, to the eyes, the nostrils, the throat,
A thin dry rain, contemptible, persistent.

In a world of definable objects, each different from each,
It unites as denominator of all,
The common agent. I see the white page
Gathering its random calligraphy under my pen,
And see at the tip of the pen the fine motes swirl
Down to that point where a fragmented earth
Silently whirls in an air choked with nothing but dust:
The pulverisation of planets, the universe dust.

CLEANING A COIN

THE green encrusted lump
Stews in its vinegar.
I peck with a pocket knife
At accretions of shell and stone.
Sand flakes from the centre.

After three days of this
The alchemy takes over.
Through a mask of verdigris
A profile stares through,
Wild-haired and chapleted.

And there on the other side
A vestigial horse capers
Across an illegible
Inscription in Greek. I rinse
The tiny disc at the tap.

I keep it now on my desk
With the other beachcombings,
This rendering down of the last
Twenty-five centuries
To a scoured chip of bleached bronze.

BUZZARDS ABOVE CYRENE

ALONE or in wheeling squadrons of dozens, they move
High above the escarpment, drift to the plain below,
The sun with a certain light obscuring their wings
So that they vanish to narrowed points of darkness
Only to swing away a moment later
Becoming spread sails, gold, brown, distinct and huge
Over tombs, junipers, red stones, red dust
Caught in a still and windless stretch of blue.
But more than that, they impose a scale by which
You measure these golden ruins, these hanging gardens of
    fossils,
These clear imperial edicts and pieties
Cluttering the ledges with magnificence,
All narrowed to points of light in an unwinking eye
For which, fathoms down, a mouse freezes still, a lizard
Flashes, a dung beetle labours through dry thorns,
Regarded, moved over like a dowser's twig,
To twitch then, jerk down, pounce, finding nothing there
But these poor small spoils, these puny snacks and beakfuls
Littered among ruins, squalid among remains,
Ravaged, scavenged, picked clean among pink blooms.

ARABIC SCRIPT

LIKE a spider through ink, someone says, mocking: see it
Blurred on the news-sheets or in neon lights
And it suggests an infinitely plastic, feminine
Syllabary, all the diacritical dots and dashes
Swimming together like a shoal of minnows,
Purposive yet wayward, a wavering measure
Danced over meaning, obscuring vowels and breath.
But at Sidi Kreibish, among the tombs,
Where skulls lodge in the cactus roots,
The pink claws breaking headstone, cornerstone,
Each fleshy tip thrusting to reach the light,
Each spine a hispid needle, you see the stern
Edge of the language, Kufic, like a scimitar
Curved in a lash, a flash of consonants
Such as swung out of Medina that day
On the long flog west, across ruins and flaccid colonials,
A swirl of black flags, white crescents, a language of swords.

CEREMONIES

In the courtyard below our balcony, a wedding;
A funeral next door. Clapping and wailing,
Steady titupping drums and the jaunty cry
Of reedy pipes: an ululation of women.
The expense and order of ceremony
Framing our notions of heaven.

Dressed in their tawdry gold, their flash brocades,
The women prepare the wedding-feast. Flies invade
Hacked sheep, green peppers, the swart blood sprinkled
And running in dusty pools. Next door
Rush mats, a flask of water, slippers, are spread
At the entrance, to be warden and purifier.

Everywhere naked light-bulbs make public
To us, looking from above, the rhetoric
Of ritual, the performed act
Done for the benefit of the sharers
And those who do not share. Two contracts
Embodied in alien observances.

In life, in death. On their hard chairs
The mourners sit, cigarettes are shared,
They wait with their formal sympathy. High,
Nasal, the tape-recorder enunciates
An accustomed, pre-recorded grief. Monotonously
The prothalamion chorus reverberates.

A small world of greetings and farewells,
Hand touching hand, lips, heart. The cooking smells
Blend with the street dust and are reconciled
As wedding guests and mourners mingle. Ceremony
Joins, fixes, hallows the strange wild
Drums in their joy, the mourners' stranger cry.

SILPHIUM

THICK-ROOTED and thick-stemmed,
Its tail embracing its stem,
Its flower-globes gathered in knots,
Now dead as the dodo,
The mastodon and the quagga,
Commemorated on coins
And in hideous Fascist fountains,
It stands as panacea
For whatever ill you choose,
Since no one living has seen it
Cure dropsy, warts, or gripe,
Flavoured a stew with it,
Or slipped it with a wink
As aphrodisiacal bait.
But there it all is in the books,
Theophrastus, Strabo, Pliny,
Fetching its weight in silver
In the market at Cyrene,
Kept in the state treasury,
Sold to equip the army
By Caesar, sent to Nero
As a rare imperial prize.
Where has it gone? The carious
Teeth of the camel, perhaps,
Have munched it away, or the goat
Scouring the dry pastures.
But I cannot credit the tough
Uncomplicated grasp
Of a plant loosening hold on life
Completely: I imagine a small
Hidden cleft in the worn rock,
Shaded by prickly pear,
Nervously footed by gecko,
Where, thick-rooted and thick-stemmed,
Its tail embracing its stem,

Those flower-globes gather in knots,
That solitary stance
Eluding the oil-prospectors,
The antiquaries, the shepherds,
Who are searching for something else
And need no panacea.

ALI BEN SHUFTI

You want coins? Roman? Greek? Nice vase? Head of god,
  goddess?
Look, shufti here, very cheap. Two piastres? You joke.

I poke among fallen stones, molehills, the spoil
Left by the archaeologists and carelessly sieved.
I am not above ferreting out a small piece
From the foreman's basket when his back is turned.
One or two of my choicer things were acquired
During what the museum labels call 'the disturbances
Of 1941': you may call it loot,
But I keep no records of who my vendors were—
Goatherds, Johnnies in berets, Neapolitan conscripts
Hot foot out of trouble, dropping a keepsake or two.
I know a good thing, I keep a quiet ear open when
The college bodysnatchers arrive from Chicago,
Florence, Oxford, discussing periods
And measuring everything. I've even done business with them:
You will find my anonymous presence in the excavation reports
When you get to 'Finds Locally Purchased'. Without a B.A.—
And unable to read or write—I can date and price
Any of this rubbish. Here, from my droll pantaloons
That sag in the seat, amusing you no end,
I fetch out Tanagra heads, blue Roman beads,
A Greek lamp, bronze from Byzantium,
A silver stater faced with the head of Zeus.
I know three dozen words of English, enough French
To settle a purchase, and enough Italian
To convince the austere *dottore* he's made a bargain.
As for the past, it means nothing to me but this:
A time when things were made to keep me alive.
You are the ones who go on about it: I survive
By scratching it out with my fingers. I make you laugh
By being obsequious, roguish, battered, in fact
What you like to think of as a typical Arab.

Well, Amr Ibn el-As passed this way
Some thirteen hundred years ago, and we stayed.
I pick over what he didn't smash, and you
Pay for the leavings. That is enough for me.
You take them away and put them on your shelves
And for fifty piastres I give you a past to belong to.

BUTTERFLIES IN THE DESERT

THROWN together like leaves, but in a land
Where no leaves fall and trees wither to scrub,
Raised like the dust but fleshed as no dust is,
They impale themselves like martyrs on the glass,
Leaving their yellow stigmata. A hundred miles
And they form a screen between us and the sparse world.
At the end of the journey we see the juggernaut
Triumphant under their flattened wings, crushed fluids.
Innocent power destroys innocent power.
But who wins, when their bloody acid eats through chrome?
In the competition for martyrs, Donatus won,
But the stout churches of his heresy now stand
Ruined, emptied of virtue, choked with innocent sand.

AT ASQEFAR

At Asqefar the German helmet
Rests like a scarecrow's bonnet
On a bare branch.
The shreds of coarse grey duffel
Hang round the gap a rifle
Left in a shallow trench.

'Much blood', said the shepherd,
Gesturing with his head
Towards the bald hillside.
A spent cartridge nestles
Among the dry thistles.
Blood long since dried.

Strange and remote, almost,
As these old figures traced
In Asqefar's cave:
There, pictured in red clay,
Odysseus comes back from Troy
Near the German's grave.

Twenty-five years since the battle
Plucked up the sand and let it settle
On the German soldier.
Far away now the living, the dead,
Disarmed, unhelmeted,
At Troy, at Asqefar.

DISTANCES

THE Gulf of Sirte: the first rim of hell.

So Ophellas of Cyrene, Ptolemy's prefect,
Led his auxiliaries, their women and children,
Like a parched glacier, a colony on the move:
Then Cato with fifteen cohorts, echoing
What Lucan wrote—'There is no green branch
To be found in all the stretch of arid sand
Between burning Leptis and torrid Bereniké'.
Poetic lie: for the camelthorn puts out
Grey tips of dry buds that the tongues of dew
Moisten to green, mocking their human thirst.

Strange breeds strike root, shallowly, under sand.
Outside Misurata, a Chinese doctor
Comes out of his Italian bungalow
(Built in the year XIV from the March on Rome)
And sees an Englishman drive by at speed
In a Volkswagen which two Bedouins try to hitch.
Distances sweep like winds across fine sand,
Lifting the margins where the map suggests
Road marked by drums, tilting towards the south
Where even the camelthorn declines to root;
Or teases us on with hope remorselessly
Like Nawfaliyah, flagged by white kilo stones
Across those distances, at last a nothing—
A gutted fort, a windpump, camels, dust.

Anno Domini nineteen-sixty-six:
Benghazi to Leptis round the Sirtic coast—
Six hundred miles, a grind of fifteen hours
In a souped-up cab smelling of peanuts and sweat.
There are no distances now,
When Severus lies in a suburb of York, or here
Where KNOX and W. GIBB have carved their names

In the white marble of the Severan Arch.
Filling their mess-tins from the water trailer,
Grinning in khaki drill around the theatre
Where Monty gave them their last pep talk, they
Are permanent, marmoreal, secure
In this close-focused telescope, history,
While Ophellas and Cato, all their cohorts,
Camp-followers, baggage, all who fell behind
And all who fell at Zem-Zem, Halfayah,
By Marble Arch and Knightsbridge, grow thick tongues
Croaking for water, and the camelthorn
Blooms in the distance like a dream of thirst.

QASĪDA ON THE TRACK TO MSUS

TOWARDS sundown we came out of the valley
Along that track
Not knowing then where it led to, when we saw
The stone circles, the heaped cairns of stone, the stones
Arranged like coracles on the dry slopes.
The brown hills were empty. Only a buzzard
Stood in the sky, perceiving its territory.

Stopping, we knew the place for an encampment
Or what remained of one: the litter of pots,
The broken shafts of ploughs, battered tin bowls,
Sickles and shears rusting, the chattels of the living.
But there were the dead too, in those stone enclosures
Laid into sand below tattered banners, marked with a stone
At head and foot. For them the tents had moved on,
The blanketed camels, the donkeys heaped high
With panniers and vessels for water. And for us too:
We had passed beyond the wells and the fresh springs
Where the goats shuffled in black congregations,
Beyond even the last dry Roman cistern before Msus
At the end of a track we never intended to take.
Behind us, the barking of dogs and the wind from the sea,
Neither concerned with us nor the way south:
In front, the steppes of gazelles and scorpions
To be hunted or burned, for those who might venture
Further into that camouflage.

But, because it was sundown, we slept there and lay
Hearing the wind, watching the rising moon
Above stars falling like snow through constellations
We could not name. At dawn, we turned back
Into the accustomed valley, a settled place,
Going between tents and herds, yelped at by dogs,
Watched by threshers and gleaners, moving among men.

And still on that hillside the ragged flags fret
Over the abandoned implements and stones,
And now I shall never reach Msus,
Having turned back to the easy valley, while those
Who were not left behind rode, I suppose, south
To some name on the map I might just recognise,
Or a day's ride beyond to a name I do not know.

THE LETTERS OF SYNESIUS

for Pablo Foster

Synesius of Cyrene: born in Libya *c.* A.D. 370, died there *c.* A.D. 413. Greek by ancestry, Roman by citizenship, he considered himself to be a Libyan, a citizen of the Libyan Pentapolis, of which Cyrene, his birthplace, was one city, and Ptolemais, of which he became bishop, was another. He studied under Hypatia at Alexandria, visited Athens, went as ambassador of the Pentapolis to Constantinople, and probably died at the hands of a native Libyan tribe, the Austuriani.

It seemed to me that I was some other person, and that I was one listening to myself amongst others who were present...
                                        SYNESIUS to HYPATIA

LETTER I

*You must know my way of speaking the truth bluntly has
followed me even to the bounds of Libya.*

                                          At Tocra
THE ephebes set hammer and chisel to the wall
Each in his different way, with different skills.
Well-oiled conscripts, glistening and drunk,
Inscribe their achievements and their names and die.
The dragon inherits the Hesperidean gardens
And spawns small lizards, quicksilver on white rock.
Lethe has lights. The dark pools breed white fish
Nevertheless, and blind white crayfish.
                                   Ask for the key
At the Military Academy where the Dean has just finished
Lecturing on the psychology of war.
The Jews have sacked Cyrene. In the tombs
Families sit round brewing tea.
                              Necropolis.
The Parliament building is locked. The wells are locked
At Gasr Lebia, where Justinian's queen
Is celebrated in mosaic: bull,
Fish, amphibious monster with a conch,
An eagle preying on a calf, crab's claws,
And perched on a curiously humped crocodile
A duck.
            The wells are dry, the drillers cry for oil
And find dry holes. Concession 65
Spouts oil and blood. Great wonders come to pass.
                                   The linguists say
The Berber cannot write but has an alphabet
No one can read. Tenders are asked
For a new road to Chad.
                         Somewhere between
Brega and Zelten, in a waste of sand,
A signpost on an oil-drum indicates
GIALO across the trackless distances.

The king is old. Undergraduates
Are taught philosophy by Egyptians now.
And at Tocra a boy indicates with gestures
How wide is Gamal Nasser's world. That face
Looks down as often as the king's, and smiles
Where the old man's is fatherly but stern.

Aristippus emigrated. There was visa trouble.
A cloud of dust in the east presages war
And the coming of the goat. Pink and yellow,
The posters proclaim in fancy Gothic script
'No word pease whill illeagal Isreil exists'
And 'Palesting was not Belfor's land to promise'
(Belfor the idolatrous, Baal the Ingilizi hound).

                              The ephebes have trouble
In mastering the Christian calendar,
The Latin alphabet. Teach us, they cry,
And go on strike. For the Franks, the wine is cheap
But when you walk the beach at the city's edge
The smashed Heineken bottles shine like grass:
Expensive mosaic. The earliest city lies here
Under this pile of donkeys' hooves. Dig here.
You find loom-weights from looms whose cloth has meshed
Into the sand, the salt, the lips of fossils.

I write between spells of guard between the watchtowers,
Or lecture on the English question-tag.

LETTER II

We have planted our fields for the fires lit by our enemies.

WE have had wise men. Where are they now? we ask.
Aristippus, who taught that pleasure was highest good,
Callimachus, writing verses in his catalogue,
And, without false modesty, myself—
Synesius, mounting guard in my bishop's cope
And watching the setting sun run creases down
The great swathe of the Jebel.
                              I have seen
The Italian farmhouses house sheep and straw,
And vv IL DUCE flake from the pink walls,
Catching the last rays of the crumbling sun.
The fourth shore's harbours clog and choke with sand.

Severus the African, speaking slow Latin
With a Berberish accent, went on campaign.
Brute tribes were pacified, our cities flourished,
But the taxes rose, the coinage was debased
So that small coins are like water in the hand.
Our emperor died on the northern frontier
And so, in time, we turn to the east.
                              What stays
Is here, where some potter from Byzantium
Has pressed on the pot's foot his full-fleshed thumb.

The language with the unpronounceable sound
Made somewhere below the glottis inherits our tongues.
'Poets are followed by none save erring men',
Said the Prophet, echoing Plato into the cave.

The ghaffir in his blanket under the stairs
Who prays five times a day to Allah the Good
Collects our garbage, has trachoma in one eye,
And shall assuredly inherit the Kingdom.

LETTER III

I would rather live a stranger among strangers.

THE slopes below the cave are thick with flints.
Here they kept ammunition in the war,
And now tether a bullock to a post
Under the eaves of rock.
                                 Places of the mind only,
Unvisited oases, tracks marked
On unreliable maps by engineers
Who saw the landscape from two thousand feet.

So it might be a god would wander
Over the landscape deserted by his people,
Looking for evidence that once they loved him.
Now they are gone. Delicate microliths
Like snowflakes litter the dry slopes, among thorns.

I am writing to you to talk about emptiness
Because this is empty country, 'where ruins flourish'.

At first you are frightened of dogs, their distant barks
Coming closer across the strewn, ungrateful rock,
And perhaps you pick up stones to shy them away.
You are right, you trespass. Take tea with them, learn the words
For 'please' and 'thank you', bark in Arabic,
Or whatever language is current at the time:
Try Berber, Greek, Latin, Turkish, Italian,
Compounds of these, gibbering dialects—
You will still sweat with fear, ducking down for stones
Which, it may be, are tools fashioned by men
Without a language.
                            To call a man a dog
Is an insult in many languages, but not to dogs.
They sniff the high octane at Benina as the planes take off,
Watching the passengers who have an hour
Between London and Nairobi, the pale transients.

Their yellow fur bristles, they yawn and snap.
At Hagfet er Rejma they patrol the tents,
Watching me glean the slopes for polished flakes.
My pockets are full, my hands are empty.
Look, dogs, how empty. This landscape is yours, not mine.

LETTER IV

Such are our celebrations, seasonable and of old tradition,
the good things of the poor.

SIMON OF CYRENE carried the cross. No Libyan
In collar and tie will carry anything.
'A proud people', says the handout wearily,
Explaining nothing.
      Lake Tritonis, place
Of Pallas Athene's birth, dries to a salt-pan
Where tin huts void their sewage. Erytheia,
Arethusa, Aegle, Hestia, are ghaffirs:
Their sweet songs are transistorised, relayed
From Radio Cairo across miles of sand.

A donkey and a microbus collide.
The donkey limps off, noisily urinates
By the side of the road, while the bus, crumpled like paper,
Waits for repairs and insurance policies.
The old survives by demanding nothing: the new
Frets in its expectations.
      I am supposed
To lead my flock through darkness until such time
As the Kingdom descends, there is no more call for martyrs,
And the meek inherit the earth. In the new order
My people go hungry thus to cleanse themselves.

In the month of Ramadan the rain begins
This year. It is December, and the stars
Wane above grey clouds, are obscured by them.
The sea is coldly feverish. Lightning streaks
The yellow stucco and the shuttered rooms.
The honey-casks, the oil-jars and the wine
Lie at the wharf. No one puts out to sea.

What can cure the soul? What food nourish it?
Fasting by day, they feast by night and cram
Sin down their gullets. In the church beyond the wall

The heretics draw lots for martyrdom.
I have nothing more to say of the good life,
Except—having seen so much—that to suppose
Things better rather than different is a way
Of dying only, swivelled to the past.
It is easy for me to act the Jeremiah,
To juxtapose the anomalous, debased present
With the golden fragments of a golden age.
The indigenous survives: the donkey limps off unhurt.
The silphium plants wilt in the private gardens
Since men no more expect a panacea.

Those who are to come will call our Lord a prophet
Mistaken among prophets. Spiritual pride
Gives way to pride of status, money, dress.
Unearth a marble goddess and you find
Her groin defiled with soldiers' filthiness.
The Temple of Zeus is smashed, the figurines
Pulped into lime. Farzúgha's church protects
A tribe of bats and owls. At Tansollúk
The arch is crammed with masonry and sand.

In the garrison chapel we sing 'God Save the Queen':
A proud people, enjoined to pray each week
For her and Johnson too.
                              Out of the sand
A scorpion heaves its fiery shoulders, smashed
By the spade, heavy with fire and venom. The old
Survives by demanding nothing: the new
Frets in its expectations. Simon bowed
Under the weight, the jeers. Something survives
As Ramadan and Christmas coincide
And we have little left to share but pride.

LETTER V

And who shall collect fruit from the desert?

THE sea licks the shore with sly assurance
Where freestone masonry tumbles in pools.
Salt will never be worm-eaten, says the proverb:
It is the eater and preserver, fixed
Like mould on the surfaces of sherds, the fabric
Coins wrap themselves in, a sharp-tongued mineral,
The taste of thirst, the desert's brother, the sea's self.

I wait for something. The facile have a saying:
If life is hard on you, dwell in cities.
Watching the sea is a lifetime's occupation,
Empty of incident: looking inland
I see not emptiness but desolation.
The cities are fallen, Barca is forked with fire,
Ashes drift down on Tocra, Cyrene lies open
Like an enormous cave laid out for looting.
Here on the other side we have the sea
Rubbing and prying and investigating,
A faceless element, unharvested.

Cretans fish sponges: red mullet fills our plates
But we do not catch them. Red earth holds spilth of seeds
But we grow little, garner less. We have a mineral
More powerful than salt, liquid as sea,
Deep in its cave for looting, to sustain us.
Why should our old men sow, our young men reap?
The tall earth-delvers feed us royalties,
Our government takes tithes. Consider Esso:
It sows not, neither does it reap. Yet was ever
Woman arrayed like this one, in the Modern
Grocery Store, trousered, in high heels? In the desert
Her man plucks golden fruit, Hesperidean
Apples whose juice flows richly to the sea
To be drunk by silver tankers.
                                    Undergraduates, you

44

Who sit your final examinations, consider
Omar Mukhtar, old man on a horse,
Who died on the gallows tortured by his wounds.
'He would have been a ghaffir now', said one
Keen student with a sneer.
                              Omar rests now,
Thirty-three years after his death, his tomb
Built like a pink carbuncle at the edge
Of Bereniké, Euhesperides,
Benghazi—cities beckoning the wise ones
Who once found life hard, who have claimed their inheritance
Out of the salt desert, the desert, the rock,
Preserver of fallen cities, of flesh, and of oil.

LETTER VI

Shut up here in our houses, then, as in a prison, we were to our regret condemned to keep this long silence.

THIS autumn I felt the cold in my bones when
In the fountain of Apollo the frogs were spawning.
Persephone was faceless. Above the Jebel
The thunder grumbled.

Fortune was elsewhere, ministering her mercies,
Dispensing luck to barbarians and atheists.
We on the coast repaired the aqueducts
But the water failed us.

Then winter came and the highways flooded,
Keeping us chained to our useless harbours,
Pent in by storms, letting our cattle
Wander uncared for.

Somewhere in the east the administrators filed us
Under a pile of disregarded papers.
We were forgotten, except by the hungry
Collector of taxes.

The Governor sends me a gilt-edged invitation
To celebrate the fourteenth year of independence.
There I shall see the outlandish consuls-general
Talking dog-Latin.

My cultivated friend, please try to send me
Whatever new books the sophists have published:
I have read the reviews in the six-month-old journals
And feel a provincial.

'We traded in shrouds: people stopped dying'.
Fortune frustrates even our death-wish.
The infant mortality figures were lost by
The census department.

Remember me now to my old friends and colleagues,
Discussing the Trinity and aureate diction:
Think of me here, awaiting the fires of
The Austuriani.

See where they squat behind the escarpment,
Ignorant of metre, of faction and schism,
Destined by favourless Fortune to be the true
Heirs of the Kingdom.

LETTER VII

I am breathing an air tainted by the decay of dead bodies. I
am waiting to undergo myself the same lot that has befallen
so many others.

LETHE, rock fissure, dark water, warm
Breath of white mist on drifting scum, not moving
Unless a white shape moves from rock to rock.
Nostrils drink steam, the air has shapes, can be touched,
Assumes phantoms. Drink here, drink, the brackish taste
On the roof of the mouth, closed with a green coin.
I am ready to descend, to enter the cave's mouth,
To put on the mist's habit, boarding the frail
Craft that has come to claim me.
                                        In 1938
The Lido at Lethe was opened to the public
And a poem by d'Annunzio was unveiled
Limned on a carefully ruined stele. Balbo
Offered full citizenship to all who filled in
The necessary forms. Electric cables
Illuminated the forgetful waters and
Two wrought-iron gates guarded oblivion.
Bertolo Giannoni at about this time
Managed to reach the grotto's far wall
And scratched his name in letters a metre high.
Perhaps by some irony he was one of those
Crushed by the tank-tracks of Keith Douglas's troop
On the way through to Agheila and Tripoli.
Bertolo survives on the wall, having drunk the waters.

The filth of pigeons, two fig trees' silver leaves,
Roots splayed from rock channels. Persephone in fossils.
He threw the switch and the sixty-watt bulbs flashed on
Too feebly to desecrate the pre-electric dark.
I walked on duck-boards over the breathing lake.
The mist came walking towards me.
                                        Death is a mystery

48

Not needing these adventitious theatricals.
In the ancient darkness the eirenic shades sleep,
Forgetting Lethe, rock fissure, dark water, warm breath.

*A camel with the mange, says the proverb, can shoulder the
burden of many asses.*

WHEN they came to ask me to serve
We were sitting over a dish of olives, drinking
Wine from Messa, the kind that tastes of stone.
We had been talking of Constantinople, the embassy
I relished so little, so far away from home.
And then they arrived, with their wallets of documents,
Their letters and seals stowed carefully away,
Their talk of Theophilus and the weather, nervously
Waiting their chance to snare me into God's acre
Before my due time. *Divine conspiracy,*
Somebody might have called it; but *duty*
Was the burden of their discourse, that
And those filial bonds they well knew bound me
To this Pentapolis, this Libya.
                     In this land
No evangelist angled for souls, no missionaries
Humped bibles along the trade routes. The sick
Children are treated by the Adventists,
The Orthodox are visited by one priest
Whose tinny bell pierces the muezzin's cry,
The quiet white nuns herd schoolgirls here and there,
And over the dust and potholes of the town
The double-breasted cathedral sits like a presence:
Mae West or Bardot, depending on your age.
The Anglicans have 'Newmarket'
Among the officers', and their ladies', horses:
The National Anthem, punkahs from Poona, words
Hallowed in Gloucestershire and Ulster, and
Hymns of the rousing sort by Wesley and Lyte.
In this whole land there is not one Christian
With a Libyan passport.
                   So I reluctantly
Accepted what they offered: Bishop, with power
Over five crumbling cities, fortress-farms,

Immitigable desert. And they accepted
My wife ('better to marry than to burn'),
My doubts, my flinching from the sweat and blood
Of trinitarian dogma. Thus I stand,
Flawed but chosen, bewildered by that choice,
Uncertain of creed, fouled in a Marian web,
Deafened by Alexandrian echoes, armed
With episcopal power in a parish of termites.
                                        Look,
At Birsis, among the rotten byres, a vaulted
Church in ruins, where a man hoes red
Soil fed with Roman water. In the rubble
A fragment shows, in frayed Greek letters, words
To the Lord, and something else I cannot read.
The servants of the Lord. Alone, he hoes and sings,
Singing to himself. Perhaps to someone else.

LETTER IX

Brought up outside the pale of the Church, and having
received an alien training, I grasped at the altars of God.

THE Dalmatians have landed their advance party
And the billeting-officer is hard at work.
I can now administer the Mass in Serbo-Croat
But the congregation is thin. I carry Christ
Like a burden on my tongue. Andronicus—
From tunny fisher's perch to governor's chariot—
Is excommunicated, but runs giddy still.
My bow sprouts mould in the yard, I have given away
My dogs, my saddle.
                              Once there was philosophy
But how can that clear stream run when I spend my days
Adjudicating ruridecanal tiffs at Hydrax or Darnis,
Squabbles about copes or the laying on of hands?
Hypatia, remember the hush in the lecture-room
When you entered serenely with your astrolabe
And began to enunciate truths?
                                        Tonight at five
A conversation-lesson with the Praetor, whose Greek
Would not fill a sardine. Yes, I am peevish.
You may say it is the climate or the place or my time of life—
But I carry a burden that was given to me
Which I do not understand. Somewhere, God's plan
Is hidden in monoliths or a wafer of bread.
His purpose obscurely works through those Slavs on the hill
As I offer his flesh and blood. Neither Gentile nor Jew
In that Kingdom. So I puzzle it out, till I hear
A knock at my study door. Come in, Praetor, come.

LETTER X

And yet this is nothing but what the ancient oracle announced as to how the Pentapolis must end.

WHAT the oracle said was vapour swathing the rock,
And we could discern a finger writing in steam
As on a tiled wall the obscene words
Doing death to life in hints and half-promises.
'Libya shall perish by the wickedness of its leaders'.
Unequivocal, you think, for the oracle?
The ambiguities are all ours—
Rumours of referendum, of abdication:
Denials of rumours, official circumlocutions:
Whispers in cafés, public demonstrations,
Restoration of order, and if necessary
The 2 a.m. visits, the executions.
I hear the same story twice, and pass on
A third version, atomised by now
To fragments with different names and places,
But still—substantially, you say—but still
The truth holds, and the whisperers hold to it.
The oracle grins like a toad, and belches fumes.

Battus stammered and lisped. Coming to ask for a voice,
He was bidden instead to build an empire. Oracle,
You are the echo of ignorance, though I believe you.
For 'abounding in fleeces' read 'running over with oil'.

Conspicuous waste, money's confederate,
Marks the economy's frontiers. Tin cans,
Bottles, bones, blood, uncollected
In a city without dustbins, demonstrate
How well we are doing.
                              The cities of the plain
Flourished as we do, but a belly-dancer
At the Riviera or the Berenice
Will hardly call God down with his dust and ashes.
Dust and ashes are what is native here,

53

Unprophesied and sempiternal. Doom
Carries a drilling-rig in a Landrover,
A geologist from Yale, and a cloud of rumour
Stinking along the salt-pans whose flamingoes
Have flown away, over whose white plateaux
The ghibli blows from the south, bringing dust to the tongue.

Andronicus, imperialist British, wily
Egyptian agitator, Zionist, Polish agent
Disguised as an engineer—you have handed over
This traduced Kingdom. Equipped for Armageddon,
The alien cavalry rides off, but in the squares
Public loudspeakers broadcast messages
Of peace, stability, spontaneous joy,
Showing how once again etcetera
And how etcetera the future is
If only we hold firm. Etcetera.

The tomb of Battus, long located here,
In fact is there. No matter. He is dead.
The archaeologists can shift him as they please.
Fires, watchtowers, fires. The oracle, asleep,
Snores in her ancient dreams, and round her head
The angels, mingling with the harpies, weep.

LETTER XI

*War and famine have not yet annihilated it completely, as
was foredoomed; but they are wearing it away and destroying
it little by little.*

HOLES in the earth, places of snakes and fleas:
We shall creep in on our bellies, we shall find refuge
Among the ignorant, the outcast, those who merit
No conquest, being too low already.
There, I suppose, we shall die.
                              This 'resurrection'
I take as allegory, for when we die,
There, in a hole like a brood of field-mice, can you
Imagine our suffocated, wasted bodies
Assuming, in some flash of lightning, wings
To make us rise, harps to be struck for joy,
And crowns to inherit the Kingdom? The Kingdom is here.

Or here, where the woman near Sirte smiles,
Smiling with stained teeth, hands red with henna,
Holding a child whose nose is running and whose ears
Are pierced for ear-rings big as saucers.
So she smiles, accustomed, poor, expecting no change.

Long before dawn the cocks are crowing here:
Their catalogue of betrayal fills the night.
At six the sky is a dome of brilliant blue,
Only at the edges furred with a grey mist
Presaging another day of burning. Who will burn?
We are not martyrs yet, and if we are
We shall not burn but be trapped in our fastnesses,
Beyond the episcopal court, the Rood, the Grail.

Hesychius, I have seen your house, its dutiful mosaics
(Where you recorded your family and our God)
Erupting like waves from centuries of rain,
Seismic disturbance, tumult of war and anthill.
The long attrition begins, the mills of God

Grind us to dust the ghibli blusters north
Into the sea where no fleet aims to fan
With Dorian sails our northward passage home.
The woman near Sirte smiles, who is to come
After barbarians, pillage, drought; and we
Are dust in the holes of the earth and under the sea.

LETTER XII

I am a minister of God, and perchance I must complete my
service by offering up my life. God will not in any case overlook
the altar, bloodless, though stained by the blood of a priest.

I HAVE reached the end. I shall write to you no more.
Dies irae is come. See the hole in heaven
The tribesmen of Cyrene showed to Battus.
I cling to the church's pillars. These are the Kingdom's last
   days.
Here are the stoups of holy water, here
The table of sacrifice. The victim is also here.

Set sail for Jedda or Jerusalem,
The miracles are due. Here is a splinter
They say is from the Rood, and here a flag
That has snuffed the air of Mecca. I leave myself
As an unholy relic, to be the dust
Neglected by the seller of souvenirs
Among his lamps, his bronzes, his rubbed coins.
Here by the shore God's altar is made whole,
Unvisited by celebrants, to be restored
By the Department of Antiquities.
Functional concrete (ruddled, grey, and brash)
Marks out what's lacking: marble, granite, wood,
The divine interstices.
                I abdicate
Having survived locust, earthquake, death
Of children, failure of crops, murrein of hopes,
And am become that ambassador in bonds
Paul spoke of.
            Now the muezzin calls his first
Exhortation, and the pillars fall.
Darkness is on the Jebel, tongues of flame
Bring ruin, not revelation. See how they lick
The rod of Aaron, Zelten's oily fires
Flaring against the night. The visions come.
The pilgrims have boarded, the pagans are at my throat.

The blood of a Greek is spilt for the blood of a Jew.
Altars are stained, a lamb is dragged by its legs
To bleed at the door of the house.
                                        Libya,
Image of desolation, the sun's province,
Compound of dust and wind, unmapped acres—
This is the place where Africa begins,
And thus the unknown, vaguer than my conjectures
Of transubstantiation, Trinity,
All those arcana for which, now, I die.

DATE DUE